INTRODUCTION
TO
ECONOMICS
AND
BUSINESS

THINGS YOU SHOULD KNOW
(QUESTIONS AND ANSWERS)

By
Rumi Michael Leigh

Introduction

I would like to thank and congratulate you for downloading this book, *"Introduction to Economics and Business, things you should know (questions and answers)"* series.

This book will give you an introduction of how economics and business work in the society. Are you a student, a business owner, both, or you plan to do something independent someday? Then this book could be of help to you.

Thanks again for downloading this book, I hope you enjoy it!

Table of Contents

Part 1: Questions

Part 1: Answers

Part 2: Questions

Part 2: Answers

Part 3: Questions

Part 3: Answers

Part 4: Questions

Part 4: Answers

Part 5: Questions

Part 5: Answers

Part 6: Questions

Part 6: Answers

Part 7: Questions

Part 7: Answers

Part 8: Questions

Part 8: Answers

Part 9: Questions

Part 9: Answers

Part 10: Questions

Part 10: Answers

Part 11: Questions

Part 11: Answers

Part 12: Questions

Part 12: Answers

Part 13: Questions

Part 13: Answers

Conclusion

Copyright

Part 1: Questions

1. What is economics?
2. What is macroeconomics?
3. What is a primary market?
4. What is a secondary market?
5. What is purchasing power?
6. Define inflation.
7. Define deflation.
8. What is a need?
9. What is a want?
10. What is labour?

Part 1: Answers

1. Economics consist of the choices people make to satisfy their needs and wants.
2. Macroeconomics is the field of economics that deals with the behaviour, structure and performance of the global economy.
3. A primary market is a market that creates new securities that is then offered to the public.
4. A secondary market is a market where the securities issued in the primary market are bought and sold.
5. Purchasing power is the ability of an individual to buy goods and services in an economy.

6. Inflation is the increase in the price level of goods and services in an economy.

7. Deflation is the decrease in the price level of goods and services in an economy.

8. A need is a necessity for survival.

9. A want is something we desire but not a necessity for survival.

10. Labour is the effort, work, dedicated to a task.

Part 2: Questions

1. What is import?
2. What is export?
3. What is a price index?
4. What is price fixing?
5. What is a price ceiling?
6. What is a price floor?
7. What is a fixed cost?
8. What is a variable cost?
9. What is a total cost?
10. What is an inventory?

Part 2: Answers

1. Import consist of goods that enter/come into a country for sale.
2. Export consist of goods that go out of a country for sale.
3. Price index shows how the average price of goods changes with time.
4. Price fixing is when one single price is set for the same good by a common agreement between firms.
5. Price ceiling is the highest price that one can legally charge for a good or service.
6. Price floor is the lowest price that one can exchange for a good and service.

7.   Fixed cost is a cost that never changes despite the quantity of goods produced.
8.   Variable cost is a cost that changes depending on the quantity of goods produced.
9.   Total cost is the addition of the fixed cost and the variable cost.
10. An inventory is a list of products for sale.

Part 3: Questions

1. What is a capital?
2. What is human capital?
3. What is public utility?
4. Give an example of a public utility service.
5. What is supply?
6. What is the law of supply?
7. What is a supply shock?
8. What is depression?
9. What is recession?
10. What is scarcity?

Part 3: Answers

1. A capital is anything of value that provides revenue.
2. Human capital is the knowledge and skill acquired through education and experience.
3. Public utility is a service provided by the state or government to the public.
4. An example of a public utility service is providing electricity.
5. Supply is the quantity of goods available.
6. The law of supply is when the supply increases when the price of the good increases.
7. A supply shock is something that causes the sudden change in the price of a good or service.
8. Depression is a long period of recession.

9. Recession is the decline in activity of an economy over a period of time.

10. Scarcity is when there is a limited amount of goods and services.

Part 4: Questions

1. Define net worth.
2. What are goods?
3. What are services?
4. Give an example of a real property.
5. Give an example of a personal property.
6. What is a shortage?
7. What is a surplus?
8. Define hyperinflation.
9. What is a shortage?
10. What is a firm?

Part 4: Answers

1. Net worth is the difference between the assets of an individual and the liabilities.
2. Goods are things produced.
3. Services are activities performed.
4. Land is an example of a real property.
5. A plane is an example of a personal property.
6. A shortage is when the demand is greater than the supply.
7. A surplus is when the supply is greater than the demand.
8. Hyperinflation is when inflation goes out of control.
9. A shortage is the excess in demand.
10. A firm is a business organisation that sells goods and services in order to make profit.

Part 5: Questions

1. What is socialism?
2. What is communism?
3. What is an asset?
4. What is a trade surplus?
5. What is a trade deficit?
6. What is balance of trade?
7. What is a mixed economy?
8. Who is an entrepreneur?
9. Who is a sole proprietor?
10. What is offshoring?

Part 5: Answers

1. Socialism is an economic system where wealth is distributed.
2. Communism is an economic system where the government makes all the decisions concerning the economy.
3. An asset is an economic resource.
4. A trade surplus is when a country exports more than it imports.
5. A trade deficit is when a country imports more than it exports.
6. Balance of trade is the difference between import and export in a country.

7. A mixed economy is a system that combines capitalism and socialism.

8. An entrepreneur is someone who starts, sets up, creates and manages a business.

9. A sole proprietor is individual who runs his own business.

10. Offshoring is when a company moves some of its operation overseas.

Part 6: Questions

1. What is an embargo?
2. What is privatization?
3. What is a Fad?
4. What is monopoly?
5. What is a cartel?
6. Define the quantity theory.
7. What is opportunity cost?
8. What is a balanced budget?
9. What is an operating budget?
10. What is consumer sovereignty?

Part 6: Answers

1. An embargo is when there is a complete restriction on the importation or exportation of a particular good.
2. Privatization is the selling of business or services formally owned and controlled by the government to investors.
3. A Fad is a short amount of time where there is a sudden increase in demand of a product.
4. Monopoly is when one seller dominates a market.
5. A cartel is when there is an agreement and cooperation between a group of producers for their interests.
6. The quantity theory is when too much money in circulation in the economy causes inflation.

7. Opportunity cost is when a benefit must be sacrificed to get something else.
8. A balanced budget is when the revenue equals spending.
9. An operating budget is the budget that covers day-to-day expenses.
10. Consumer sovereignty is the power a consumer processes to decide the thing that gets produced in the society.

Part 7: Questions

1. What is cost/benefit analysis?
2. What is a stock?
3. Who are stockholders?
4. What is a dividend?
5. What is a demand curve?
6. What is a bond?
7. What is marginal cost?
8. What is marginal benefit?
9. What is a charter?
10. What is a conglomerate?

Part 7: Answers

1. Cost/benefit analysis is the decision made when one considers the sacrifice and goals when he takes certain actions.
2. A stock is a share of ownership of a company.
3. Stockholders are people who own a share or shares in a stock of a corporation.
4. A dividend is the money paid by a company out of its profits to its shareholders.
5. A demand curve is a graph that represents the relationship between the price and demand at a given time.
6. A bond is money loaned to an entity for a period of time.
7. Marginal cost is the cost of adding one product.

8. Marginal benefit is the extra benefit of adding one product.

9. A charter is a written government approval in order for a corporation to be established.

10. A conglomerate is two or more corporations engaged in different businesses that are in one corporate group.

Part 8: Questions

1. What is structural unemployment?
2. What is unlimited life?
3. What are substitutes?
4. What are complements?
5. What is the learning effect?
6. What is competition?
7. What is a cooperative?
8. What is a collusion?
9. What is a default?

Part 8: Answers

1. Structural unemployment is when the skills of a person looking for a job does not match the job's requirements.
2. Unlimited life is the continuity of a corporation even when it's ownership changes.
3. Substitutes are products that can be used instead of other products.
4. Complements are products that tend to be used together.
5. The learning effect indicates that more education yields higher income.
6. Competition is a rivalry between two or more entities to achieve something.
7. Cooperative is a group of people working together for a benefit.

8. A collusion is a secret agreement between people.
9. A default is when a debtor fails to make a payment past the deadline.

Part 9: Questions

1. What is fiat money?
2. What is principal?
3. What is elasticity?
4. What is demand elasticity?
5. What is the law of demand?
6. What is rationing?
7. What is predatory pricing?
8. What is an incentive?
9. What is a vertical merger?
10. What is total expenditure?

Part 9: Answers

1. Fiat money is a type of currency made legal by the government.
2. Principal is the original investment.
3. Elasticity is the relationship between quantity and price.
4. Demand elasticity is the point where the change in price causes a change in demand.
5. The law of demand is when more of a product is bought when the price is lower than higher.
6. Rationing is the control of the distribution of goods and services in order to deal with scarcity.

7. Predatory pricing is the selling of a product below the cost of production for a short period of time in order to chase out competitors.
8. An incentive is something that motivates us to do a task.
9. A vertical merger is the combination of firms that occupies the different stages of marketing or manufacturing.
10. Total expenditure is the total amount of money spent on a product.

Part 10: Questions

1. What is a free enterprise system?
2. What is barter?
3. What is a merger?
4. What is market equilibrium?
5. What is oligopoly?
6. What is a derived demand?
7. What is unlimited liability?
8. What is subsidy?
9. What is a monopolistic competition?
10. What is a non-price competition?

Part 10: Answers

1. A free enterprise system is a system where the market is mainly regulated through private means rather than political means.
2. Barter is the exchange of goods or services.
3. A merger is when two or more businesses are combined to form a firm.
4. Market equilibrium is when there is an equal demand and supply in a market.
5. Oligopoly is a market in which the producers do not have any control of the market.
6. A derived demand is how a change in customer preference affects the market.

7. Unlimited liability is when the owner of a business is fully responsible for all the debts and losses.

8. Subsidy is a benefit given to an individual, business, etc primarily by the government.

9. Monopolistic competition is an imperfect competition in which firms have many competitors but they sell a product that is slightly different.

10. A non-price competition is when competitors in the market do other things to beat their competitors instead of bringing down the price of their products like making better designs, advertisement, etc.

Part 11: Questions

1. What is a stock exchange?
2. Who is a stockbroker?
3. What is excise tax?
4. What is a market?
5. What is a free market economy?
6. What is a commodity?
7. What is a share?
8. What is a horizontal merger?
9. What is a corporation?
10. What are non-profit organizations?

Part 11: Answers

1. A stock exchange is where stocks are bought and sold.
2. A stockbroker is a person that connects buyers and sellers of stock.
3. Excise tax is the tax on a good either produced or sold.
4. A market is a system where there is exchange of goods and services between buyers and sellers.
5. A free market economy is when business transactions between buyers and sellers are done only with the mutual agreements of the two parties.
6. A commodity is an interchangeable good or material.
7. A share is a portion of stock.

8. A horizontal merger is the combination of firms that produce the same kind of product.
9. A corporation is a business structure that has a legal existence to act as a single entity.
10. Non-profit organizations are organisations exempt of income tax that provides public benefit.

Part 12: Questions

1. Define standard of living.
2. What is the labour force?
3. What is a labour union?
4. What is a patent?
5. What is net income?
6. What is a household?
7. What is a general partnership?
8. What is a limited partnership?
9. What is a franchise?
10. What is a business licence?

Part 12: Answers

1. Standard of living is a measure of wealth and comfort of individuals in a country.
2. The labour force consists of employed or unemployed people.
3. A labour union is an organization that aims to improve the working conditions for its members.
4. A patent is the licence given to the creator of a new product, exclusive rights to sell the product for a certain period of time.
5. Net income is the profit after subtracting all expenses from revenue.

6. A household involves a person or more living in the same roof.

7. A general partnership is a kind of partnership in which all the partners have equal responsibilities in the management of the business.

8. A limited partnership is the kind of partnership where one or more partners have limited responsibilities in running the business.

9. A franchise is the authority given to someone by an organisation that permits the person to take part in certain operations in the organisation.

10. A business licence is the right issued by the government to run a business.

Part 13: Questions

1. What is an aggregate supply?
2. What is an aggregate demand?
3. What is a mortgage?
4. What is a debit card?

Part 13: Answers

1. An aggregate supply is the total supply of goods and services produced by an economy over a period of time.
2. An aggregate demand is the total amount of goods and services demanded in an economy over a period of time.
3. A mortgage is a loan used to buy a house.
4. A debit card is a card that is used to withdraw money from a bank account.

Conclusion

Thank you once again for downloading this book. I hope it has given you more insights in economics and business.

Please, if you enjoyed this book, I would like you to leave a review. It'd be appreciated.

Thank you.

Copyright

Copyright © 2020 Rumi Michael Leigh